the pause.

learning to seek God

This Book Belongs To:

Date:

Powered by: LeaderTreks

The Pause: Learning To Seek God
© 2010, 2011 by youth**ministry**360

Published by LeaderTreks in the United States of America.

ISBN 13: 978 1 935832 133
ISBN 10: 1 935832 13 1

Author: Andy Blanks
Design: Upper Air Creative
Copy Editor: Lynn Groom

CONTENTS

STEP ONE . . .

Every journey begins with a single step. And you're about to embark upon a journey, of sorts. This journey will lead you to look at your life and faith from perspectives you might not have ever considered before.

Like all journeys, it has the potential to be an awesome experience. But a lot of the value of this experience depends on you.

HAVE YOU PREPARED FOR THE JOURNEY?

Ask yourself: Am I in the right mindset? Is my heart prepared to hear God's voice? Am I willing to be changed? If you can't answer "yes" to these questions, this journey might not be nearly as spectacular as it could be. If you need to, take a moment and silently talk to God in prayer. Ask God to give you a heart that is open to His leading.

YOU'RE HOLDING YOUR MAP

This book you're holding is the roadmap for your journey. It will help guide your experiences. Hold on to it. Write your name and the date in the front. If this journey turns out to be as meaningful as it could potentially be, you'll want to look back and remember this time in your life.

MAKE AN IMPACT, BE IMPACTED

As you start your journey, keep your eyes and ears open for those valuable moments where God seems to speak to you. But don't miss the chance you have to impact your fellow travelers. And to be impacted by them. Your friends are with you in this experience. Be open to what God is doing in and through them, and how He might be using them to speak to you. And vice versa.

Your journey is beginning.

Be prepared to be changed . . .

The Pause SESSION 1 INTRO

What do you do with all your free time?

If you're like most teenagers, you're
saying, "WHAT FREE TIME?"

Your generation is busier and more involved than any generation before
you. School, work, clubs, sports, friends, band, church . . . you name it,
you're involved in it.

And when you *do* have down time, you're watching YouTube™ on your
phone, playing video games, texting your friends, hitting Facebook. . .
all while watching some reality TV show.

Let's just be honest: You're not finding a lot of downtime to spend
growing your relationship with God.

And when you *do* have time, there is so much "noise" from all the
entertainment at your fingertips that you can't focus.

THIS STUDY IS ABOUT SLOWING
DOWN AND FOCUSING.

THIS STUDY IS ABOUT HITTING **PAUSE**.

YOU'RE ABOUT TO LEARN WHY IT'S IMPORTANT TO MAKE TIME TO
GROW YOUR RELATIONSHIP WITH GOD. AND YOU'RE ABOUT TO
LEARN EXACTLY HOW TO DO THIS.

ARE YOU READY?

LET'S GET STARTED . . .

Large Group SESSION 1 NOTES

Session 1 Title: Hitting Pause

These two pages are designed for you to take notes during Large Group Sessions. The stuff you're learning tends to build on itself over the next few sessions. So, even if you're not much of a note taker, you might want to at least jot down what you think is important.

Try writing down:
- Any specific teaching points
- Quotes that make you think
- Verse references for Scripture passages
- Anything you have a question about

Small Group SESSION 1 INTRO

You've been introduced to this concept of hitting pause.

Hopefully, you have begun to catch a glimpse of how vital hitting pause is to your relationship with God.

Hopefully you have grasped that hitting pause and making time for God is vital to your faith life.

But here's the deal . . . Until you truly begin to understand and value just how important it is to hit pause on a regular basis, you will never change your behavior.

You have to believe something is important before you do something about it.

So, the question is . . . Right now . . . today . . . is growing closer to God important to you?

Before you answer, what do your actions say?

If you want to grow closer to God, you're in the right place. Get ready to be challenged. But get ready to be equipped, too.

What are you waiting on?
Let's get started . . .

SESSION 1: GETTING STARTED

Work with your small group leader to respond to the following stats.

Are you busy? Overcommitted? Feel like you have a lot going on?

You're not alone. Research conducted on US teenagers paints an interesting picture of your life. You're busy. And you're stressed. Check out the stats below:

Seventy-eight percent of teenagers identify schoolwork as the number one source of stress in their lives. FORTY-ONE PERCENT OF TWELFTH GRADERS PARTICIPATE IN SOME FORM OF PERFORMING ARTS, SUCH AS DANCE, BAND, ART, OR THEATER.

Fifty percent of all 16- to 19-year-olds have a job or are looking for work.

NEARLY EIGHT MILLION TEENAGERS PLAY HIGH SCHOOL SPORTS.

At least when you're not in school or at work or at practice, you have time to rest. Um . . . not so much.

Check out this quote from a major study on teenagers and media use: The average American teenager "spends practically every waking minute—except for the time in school—using a smart phone, computer, television or other electronic device."

Fifty percent of teenagers send 50 or more text messages a day. Thirty percent send more than 100 texts a day.

NEARLY SEVENTY-THREE PERCENT OF ALL TEENAGERS USE SOCIAL NETWORKING SITES.

Seventy-six percent of all teenagers own an iPod or an MP3 player.

ON THE AVERAGE DAY, THE AVERAGE 18-YEAR-OLD SPENDS:
• 4.5 hours watching TV . . . • 2.5 hours listening to music or audio . . . • 1.5 hours on the computer . . . • A little over an hour playing video games . . . • Around half an hour reading and half an hour watching movies . . . • For a total of 10 hours and 45 minutes of media exposure a day.

SESSION 1: DIGGING IN

Ready to learn about hitting Pause? Follow your leader's instructions to work through these questions with your group.

Describe what happens when you "hit pause."

LET'S SEE WHAT WE CAN LEARN FROM LOOKING AT JESUS' ATTITUDE TOWARD HITTING PAUSE.

Read Mark 1:32-38. Then answer the following questions:

- **How does Mark describe the place that Jesus went?**

- **What did Jesus do when He was alone?**

Read Mark 6:45-47. Then answer the following questions:

- **Describe exactly what verses 45-47 show Jesus doing.**

- **So, let's summarize these verses. What general characteristics of hitting pause can we learn from looking at Jesus' example?**

NOW LET'S SEE WHAT WE CAN LEARN FROM OTHER PEOPLE IN THE BIBLE ABOUT SEEKING GOD BY HITTING PAUSE:

Read Psalm 5:3. Then answer the following questions:

- **What do we know about the priority David put on hitting pause?**

- **Describe what we know about David's attitude as he spent time with God.**

Read Daniel 6:10. Then answer the following question:

- **What can we tell about how important Daniel's relationship with God was?**

Read Acts 10:9. Then answer the following questions:

- **What does Peter's habits and attitude toward hitting pause have in common with these other accounts?**

FINALLY, LET'S BRING ALL OF THIS HOME . . .

- If you compared your attitude toward making time to be with God with the other examples you just read, how do you stack up?

- What is the most notable difference in how you approach "hitting pause," and how these individuals approached it?

- As we begin to really consider how to apply these concepts in our lives, we have to believe they are important.
  - o In your mind, why is it important to make time for relationship with God in solitude and silence?
  - o What is the purpose?

How do the following verses speak to God's purpose for our lives?

"You are the salt of the earth. But if the salt loses its saltiness, how can it be made salty again? It is no longer good for anything, except to be thrown out and trampled by men. You are the light of the world. A city on a hill cannot be hidden. Neither do people light a lamp and put it under a bowl. Instead they put it on its stand, and it gives light to everyone in the house. In the same way, let your light shine before men, that they may see your good deeds and praise your Father in heaven." (Matt. 5:13-16)

How does knowing how and when to "hit pause" help you fulfill your God-given purpose?

SESSION 1: WRAPPING UP

What's in your way? Read this quote with your group and consider the following questions.

Our religious activities should be ordered in such a way as to leave plenty of time for the cultivation of the fruits of solitude and silence. A.W. Tozer

- Does this describe your spiritual life? (Don't feel bad if it doesn't. You're not alone.)

- Describe your spiritual life in two words: _____

- Why is it so stinking hard to just slow down and make room to be still and quiet?

- Think about this: what if God has been speaking to you, but you haven't heard Him because you haven't been listening?

Think for a minute. . . . What are the "noisy" things in your life that get in the way of spending silent time alone with God? Circle the objects below that present the biggest challenge.

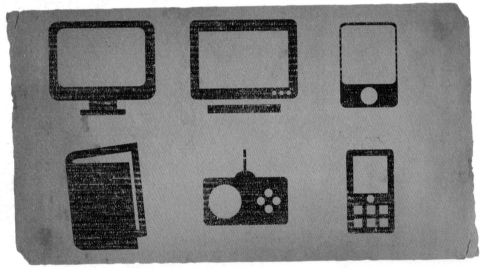

Here's a question: If you know that these things keep you from silent time with God, why don't you do something about it?

Try this: Make a commitment to take a 15- to 30-minute break from the two or three biggest noise makers in your life. Use the silence to study the Bible or talk with God in prayer. You'll be surprised at how rewarding it is.

SESSION 2 INTRO

How important are relationships to you?

PRETTY IMPORTANT, RIGHT?

What if you only talked to a parent or a friend once every couple of weeks? Would you stay close? Would you still know what was going on in their lives?

OF COURSE, NOT. TO BE CLOSE TO PEOPLE WE HAVE TO COMMUNICATE WITH THEM.

SO, WHY IS IT THAT WE THINK WE CAN HAVE A RELATIONSHIP WITH CHRIST AND ONLY TALK TO HIM EVERY ONCE IN A WHILE? LIKE ANY RELATIONSHIP, YOUR RELATIONSHIP WITH THE LORD HAS TO BE CULTIVATED AND MAINTAINED. YOU HAVE TO *WANT* TO GROW CLOSER TO HIM. AND YOU HAVE TO MAKE TIME TO TALK WITH HIM.

THIS CLOSENESS COMES THROUGH PRAYER. IF HITTING PAUSE IS ABOUT THE RELATIONSHIP BETWEEN YOU AND GOD, THEN PRAYER IS THE LANGUAGE OF THIS RELATIONSHIP.

And this session, session 2, is all about this language.

10

LARGE GROUP SESSION 2 NOTES

SESSION 2 TITLE: TALK THE TALK
These two pages are designed for you to take notes during
Large Group Sessions. The stuff you're learning tends to build
on itself over the next few sessions. So, even if you're not much
of a note taker, you might want to at least jot down what you
think is important.

Try writing down:
• Any specific teaching points
• Quotes that make you think
• Verse references for Scripture passages
• Anything you have a question about

Small Group SESSION 2 INTRO

Prayer is the language of your relationship with God.

Has that sunk in yet?

Have you grasped how truly vital prayer is? Or is it something you take for granted?

Jesus' disciples had a good idea that prayer was important. They figured they needed to be on the same page as Jesus when it came to prayer. So, they asked Him.

"Teacher, how are we supposed to pray?"

Jesus did not let them down. He gave them an awesome model for communicating with God. In this section, we'll be looking at this model and how to apply it to our lives.

The question for you is, "Are you as concerned with prayer that pleases God as the disciples were?"

Maybe it's time you gave your prayer life a closer look to see if it lines up with what God desires from you.

Now's a great time to do it . . .

SESSION 2: GETTING STARTED

How Well Do You Know Your BFF? Answer the following questions about your BFF. See who knows their best friend the best!

What is your BF's favorite kind of junk food?

Where is your BF's favorite place to hang out?

If your BF could spend one day with a celebrity, who would it be?

What is one weird or slightly annoying habit your BF has?

What is the best song your BF has on his or her iPod?

What is the worst song your BF has on his or her iPod?

What does your BF want to be when he or she grows up?

SESSION 2: DIGGING IN

It's time to get serious about prayer! Work with your leader and your group to learn all about Jesus' model of prayer.

SOME THINGS TO THINK ABOUT:
- What tone of voice do you use to pray? Is it friendly? Is it formal?
- How is your tone influenced by how you view God? (In other words, are you too formal with God because you're scared of Him? Or are you too conversational with Him?)
- What elements make up the majority of your prayers? Are you asking for stuff? Praying for others? Praising Him? Confessing?
- How many times a week are you having meaningful times of prayer with God?
- Do you ever feel like you want to pray but don't know how?

READ MATTHEW 6:9-13 AND WORK THROUGH THE DIFFERENT SECTIONS OF THE LORD'S PRAYER AS A GROUP.

PART 1:

- How does knowing that you're approaching God as a child would approach a loving father change your prayers?

PART 2:

- What role can you have in playing a part in seeing God's will done on this earth?

- What does praying for specific needs in the lives of others have to do with God's will being done on this earth?

PART 3: _____

- Give a list of some of your daily needs.

- What is the difference between a need and a want?

PART 4: _____
_____

- Why do we need forgiveness from God?

- Why is it important for us to forgive others?

PART 5: _____
_____

- Why is it so hard for us to resist the temptation to do things that are against God's will?

SESSION 2: WRAPPING UP

Take some time to yourself to practice this model of praying. Follow your leader's instructions and be ready to talk about the experience when you're done.

PART 1: PRAISE GOD The first thing we do when we pray is to praise God. In the space below, tell God He is great. Praise Jesus for His sacrifice. Thank God for His blessings.

_____

_____

_____

PART 2: OPEN MY EYES God is at work and He's chosen you to be a part of His plan. In the space below, ask God to open your eyes to the opportunities around you where He can use you.

_____

_____

_____

PART 3: ASK YOUR FATHER God knows what you need. He promises to meet your needs. In the space below, write how God has met your needs in the past. Then, take your needs to God. Trust Him to meet them.

_____

_____

_____

PART 4: SEEK AND GIVE MERCY If you believe in Christ, your sins are forgiven. God expects you to forgive others, also.
Confess your sins to God. Thank Him for forgiving you. Then pray about those you need to forgive.

PART 5: GIVE ME STRENGTH God never causes us to sin. . . . God promises to give us strength when we're tempted.
In the space below, ask God to give you the strength to resist temptation. Thank Him in advance for providing you with His strength.

_____

_____

_____

BEFORE YOU FINISH . . .
One of the most important aspects of praying is listening . . .
As you close your prayer, simply be quiet and reflect on this time. God will speak to you through your thoughts, your circumstances, and His Word. Patiently listen to Him . . .

SESSION 3 INTRO

In the last lesson, you learned that prayer is the language of your relationship with God.

This is true.

BUT HOW CAN YOU TALK TO SOMEONE YOU DON'T KNOW?

What if you only talked to a parent, or a friend once every couple of weeks? Would you stay close? Would you still know what was going on in their lives?

THE TRUTH IS, YOU CAN'T.

Prayer is a major component of **hitting pause**. But Bible study is equally important. The Bible is the main way that God has chosen to make Himself known to us.

Sure, we can get to know God through other ways . . .

. . . THROUGH HIS CREATION.

. . . THROUGH OUR EXPERIENCES.

. . . THROUGH THE HOLY SPIRIT.

. . . EVEN THROUGH OUR RELATIONSHIPS WITH OTHER, WISER CHRIST-FOLLOWERS.

BUT THE BIBLE IS GOD'S MAIN WAY OF PROVIDING YOU A WAY TO GET TO KNOW HIM.

Do you want to know the Bible better? Does it sometimes confuse you? Not sure where to start or what to do once you get there? If you answered yes to any of these questions, you're in the right place.

Large Group SESSION 3 NOTES

Session 3 Title: Knowing The Bible

These two pages are designed for you to take notes during Large Group Sessions. The stuff you've learned has built on itself over the last two sessions. So, even if you're not much of a note taker, you might want to at least jot down what you think is important.

Try writing down:
- Any specific teaching points
- Quotes that make you think
- Verse references for Scripture passages
- Anything you have a question about

Small Group SESSION 3 INTRO

Think for a minute about what you would be if you could be anything in the world.

Seriously. Let your mind go nuts.

What would you be?

CENTERFIELDER FOR THE BOSTON RED SOX?

A PEDIATRICIAN WORKING IN THE SLUMS OF AFRICA OR SOUTHEAST ASIA?

A GRAMMY AWARD WINNING POP-DIVA?

A DANCER? A COWBOY? A TEACHER? AN ENGINEER?

Whatever it is you're dreaming of, imagine there was a book that told you the "in's and out's" of it. All you had to do was read it, and you could have all the knowledge you would need to be exactly what you want to be.

When it comes to your life as a Christ-follower, the Bible pretty much works this way!

God has given you all you need to know about Him, His ways, His work throughout history, and the guidance you need to live like one of His children.

This lesson will help you know exactly how to dig-in to this awesome book.

(Trouble is, after this lesson . . . you won't have an excuse for not reading it any more!)

LET'S GET STARTED . . .

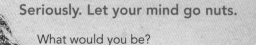

SESSION 3: GETTING STARTED

If you're a Christ-follower, the Bible is supposed to be a big part of your life. But is it? Take the quiz to find out!

Your leader will read out several questions. Each question has a different point value. For each question, write out your answer's point value in the space provided. Then, tally up your scores using the answer chart below.

Question 1:

Question 2:

Question 3:

Question 4:

Question 5:

WHAT'S YOUR TOTAL SCORE? _____

Now look at the key below. What does your score say about how important your Bible is to you?

20-17 points You and your Bible are really tight.
16-12 points You're on the right track.
11-7 points The Bible doesn't appear to be that important to you.
6-0   points Yikes! You have virtually zero interaction with the Word.

SESSION 3: DIGGING IN

What does it look like when you really know the Bible? Work with your leader and your group to find out.

WHAT DOES IT LOOK LIKE WHEN YOU KNOW YOUR BIBLE?

WHAT DOES IT LOOK LIKE WHEN YOU DON'T KNOW YOUR BIBLE?

1. Knowing the Bible equals

   _____

   the Bible. (Psalm 119:97)

1.

2. Knowing the Bible gives you

   _____ and

   _____ when it

   comes to the world around

   you. (Psalm 119:98-100)

2.

3. Knowing the Bible leads to

   a life of _____.
   (Psalm 119:101-103)

3.

4. Knowing the Bible equals

   knowing _____

   _____.

   (Psalm 119:104)

4.

Ignorance of the Scripture is ignorance of Christ.
— ST. JEROME

SESSION 3: WRAPPING UP, PART 1
MEDITATION IN "THE PAUSE"

Let's put our knowledge to work! Follow your leader's instructions to give "meditating" on God's Word a try.

In Psalm 1, David described a blessed man by saying:

> *"His delight is in the law of the LORD,*
> *and on his law he meditates day and night."*

Meditating on God's Word is simple. Basically you read it and think about it. (Told you it was simple.) Let's practice a bit . . .

Turn in your Bibles to Romans 8:38-39. Read the passage slowly.

STEP 1 Clear your thoughts and pray that the Holy Spirit will help you see God's truth in this passage.

STEP 2 Read the passage again, thinking about what each word is saying.

STEP 3 Clear your head of any distractions. Now read the verses one last time, focusing on words that jump out at you. You may choose to circle these words or phrases, or write them in a journal.

Now ask yourself these questions:
- How do these verses make you *feel*?
- What do you want to say to God after reading this?
- How might these verses change your outlook on your day or your life?

Finally, pray to God thanking Him for what He has shown you through His Word.

There, you just meditated on God's Word. Pretty cool, right? Use this sheet as a model to help you meditate on God's Word as you "hit pause."

MEDITATION

SESSION 3: WRAPPING UP, PART 2
MINING IN "THE PAUSE"

Meditation is one aspect of interacting with God's Word as you hit pause. But there's another way, too. Follow your leader's instructions to experience "mining" God's Word.

Meditating on God's Word is important. But mining is, too. Mining is searching the depths of God's Word for a greater understanding of specific passages. Let's give it a shot.

STEP 1: Read the passage.
- Read Ephesians 2:4-5.
- Read it again, paying attention to what stands out as important.
- Write down your thoughts or questions below.

_____

_____

_____

_____

[NOTE: If you have questions, now is the time to answer them. Search for key words in the concordance in the back of your Bible, or ask your parents, youth worker, or another adult you trust.]

STEP 2: Know the context.
- Go back a few verses before the passage you're studying. Read until you come to your passage.
- Now read a few verses past your passage. You should have a better idea of what's going on now.

STEP 3: Find the main idea.
- Write what you think is the main idea for Ephesians 2:4-5.

_____

_____

_____

STEP 4: Live the truth.
- The Bible must influence your life. Live out the main truth of this passage today.

MINING

SESSION 4 INTRO

HITTING PAUSE AND SPENDING TIME WITH GOD IS A GREAT THING.

In fact, hopefully you know by now that it's a vital component in your relationship with God.

Hitting pause and taking time out to be alone with God is an incredible way of focusing on your *personal* relationship with Him. It's a way of looking inward and allowing God to fill you with His Spirit and His understanding.

BUT, YOU CAN'T STAY THERE.

God expects you to live life in "play," not in "pause."

You see, hitting pause focuses on you. **But hitting play** focuses on others . . . others in this world who desperately need to hear God's message of unconditional love and peace.

GOD HAS CHOSEN YOU TO BE HIS MESSENGER.

You have to make time to hit pause.

But hitting play and living your life as a Christ-follower . . . that's what life is all about.

AND THAT'S WHAT THIS FINAL SECTION OF **THE PAUSE** IS ABOUT.

LARGE GROUP SESSION 4 NOTES

SESSION 4 TITLE: HITTING PLAY
These two pages are designed for you to take notes during Large Group Sessions. You've come a long way so far. Don't give up now! Even if you're not much of a note taker, you might want to at least jot down what you think is important.

Try writing down:
- Any specific teaching points
- Quotes that make you think
- Verse references for Scripture passages
- Anything you have a question about

Small Group SESSION 4 INTRO

Think about those people who perform best on the biggest stage, with the most riding on it . . .

THE ATHLETE WHO COMES THROUGH WITH THE BIG HIT OR THE BIG SHOT.

THE DOCTOR WHO SAVES THE LIFE OF A PATIENT IN THE NICK OF TIME.

THE SINGER WHO HITS THE HIGH NOTE FOR THE BIG FINISH.

How do all of these individuals perform so well when the stakes are the highest?

In every situation, it's what they did before the big moment that allows them to excel when it matters most.

The guy who gets the big hit in the bottom of the 9th can only do so because he has taken thousands of practice swings preparing for such a moment.

You know . . . if you think about it, your spiritual life is the same way.

The time you spend "hitting pause" is like practicing for the big game.

But here's an interesting question:

Do you know what to do when the big game comes? Do you know what's expected of you when it matters most?

You're about to find out.

SESSION 4: GETTING STARTED

So, how unprepared have you been in your life? Follow your leader's instructions to see if you can guess who among you has made the biggest goof from being unprepared.

SESSION 4: DIGGING IN

You know the importance of hitting pause. But what is your life supposed to look like when you hit play? Work with your leader and group to find out!

WHAT KIND OF LIFE DOES "HITTING PAUSE" PREPARE YOU FOR? WHAT DOES A LIFE LIVED IN "PLAY" LOOK LIKE?

Living Life In Play Means: Knowing Your Identity

- Read 2 Corinthians 5:17. What does this verse say about your identity?

- What does it mean to be "in Christ"?

- How does this new identity impact who you are on a daily basis?

Living Life In Play Means: Knowing Your Mission

- Read 2 Corinthians 5:18-19. What word jumps out at you?

- What does the word *reconcile* mean?

- Verse 18 says God did two things. What were they?

- In your own words, what does it mean that your mission is to carry the message of reconciliation (vs. 19)?

- How does this affect your daily life?

Living Life In Play Means: Knowing Your Role

- What does verse 20 say about your role?

- In your own words, what does it mean to be an ambassador?

- What does it mean that we are Christ's ambassadors on this earth?

ARE YOU A MESSENGER?

Think about the people represented in the categories below. How are you engaging these people with the message of Christ's reconciliation?

STRANGERS

PEERS

PEOPLE YOU ENCOUNTER BUT MAY NOT KNOW.

OTHER TEENS AT SCHOOL OR WORK

FRIENDS

CLASSMATES

TEAMMATES

INNER CIRCLE
FAMILY
CLOSE FRIENDS

SESSION 4: WRAPPING UP

How effective are you at being a "messenger of reconciliation"? Work with your leader and your group to get an idea of how effective you all are at getting the message out.

HERE'S YOUR CHANCE TO BE HONEST WITH YOURSELF AND TAKE STOCK OF YOUR ACTIONS AND ATTITUDES.

Answer the questions below . . . But be honest!

1. Briefly describe the last time you had a meaningful discussion about God, or spiritual things with someone whom you know doesn't have a relationship with Christ.

2. What are the main obstacles keeping you from having real, honest conversations about God and faith with people?

3. OK, so you're God's messenger. Do you feel like you know the message well enough to really represent it? If not, are you willing to finally do something about it? What can you do to learn the message better?

4. Can you list the initials of three or four people you know need to hear the message of God's love for them?

5. What will it take for you to commit to talking to these people about God?

CLOSING

You've been given a lot of knowledge over the course of Pause.

You've learned the importance of making time to spend with God . . . alone . . . separated from the noise of the world.

You've learned the importance of prayer. More importantly, you learned how to use the Lord's Prayer as a model for your interactions with God.

You've learned the importance of knowing the Bible . . . Basically, it's how we know God. You've also learned how to meditate on and mine Scripture, valuable skills you can take with you as you grow in your faith.

Finally, you've learned what a life lived in play looks like. You know that you are called to be focused on bringing the life-changing message of Christ and His love to those who most need it.

You've learned a lot.

The question is, "What will you do with it?

Don't miss the opportunity to put the knowledge you've learned into practice. Be brave enough to make the changes in your life necessary to grow deeper in your relationship with the Lord.

Make time to hit pause. Take the initiative to live in play. The impact the Lord will make on this world through you is worth every ounce of your effort.

PAUSE DEVOTION 1

Think about your day. In school your brain works all day. You might hang out at lunch, but maybe you cram for a test. After school you have practice. Or clubs. Or church. Or a job.

In the evening you have homework. Maybe you skip the homework and go watch TV. Or get on Facebook. Or play a video game. (Or all of them at the same time!) When you're finally done with your day, you might fire off a last minute text to a friend and watch TV until you fall asleep.

It's a busy life, isn't it? Do you find yourself wishing you had more quiet time to spend with God? Do you find yourself wanting to get closer to God in prayer and in His Word? If you do, this fact may add even more stress to your life—stress that already exists because of how busy you are.

Jesus understood that this world will wear you out. It will cause you anxiety. See what He said in Matthew 11:28-29:

"Come to me, all you who are weary and burdened, and I will give you rest. Take my yoke upon you and learn from me, for I am gentle and humble in heart, and you will find rest for your souls."

We can't find spiritual rest unless we intentionally, deliberately make time to quiet all the distractions around us and hit pause. To grow deeper and more in love with God, you have to find an atmosphere of silence and peacefulness. With just God and you.

SOMETHING TO THINK ABOUT . . .

1. Ask yourself this question, and take a moment to truly think about the answer: Do you really want to grow closer to God? Seriously. . . don't rush through this. In your heart, is a closer relationship with God important to you?

2. If you answered "yes" to the previous question, answer this question: What do you think the one or two biggest obstacles to you growing closer to God are?

3. What will it take for you to address these obstacles? If you are serious about wanting to get closer to God, what is keeping you from doing what it takes to make it happen?

4. If you answered "no" to the first question, what do you attribute this to? Is this something that causes you some discomfort? If you want to grow closer to God but lack the desire, would you consider talking to your youth minister or another adult about your feelings?

PAUSE DEVOTION 2

Hopefully you had an awesome experience learning how to use the Lord's Prayer as a model to pray. And hopefully you had a chance to actually practice it. While we're on the subject, let's take another moment to think about prayer.

You're going to take one more look at prayer, this time through the words of Jesus in Matthew 7:7-11. In verses 7-8, Jesus said the following:

"Ask and it will be given to you; seek and you will find; knock and the door will be opened to you. For everyone who asks receives; he who seeks finds; and to him who knocks, the door will be opened."

When you see the word ask here, what should you think of? Think of prayer! The picture Jesus was painting was the picture of prayer as the language of our relationship with God.

But check out verses 9-11.
"Which of you, if his son asks for bread, will give him a stone? Or if he asks for a fish, will give him a snake? If you, then, though you are evil, know how to give good gifts to your children, how much more will your Father in heaven give good gifts to those who ask him!"

Do you see it? This is all about relationship! Jesus compared God, our heavenly Father, to our earthly fathers. If you're starving and ask one of your parents for bread, will they give you a rock? No. Now some of your mom's cooking might taste like dirt, but that's beside the point.

What Jesus was saying was that we're God's children. And when we go to Him in prayer, He answers our prayers, providing exactly what we need.

When we pray to God, and He doesn't seem to answer our prayers the way we want, maybe we need to rethink what we're asking for. Maybe it isn't a need after all. Or maybe He just hasn't provided it yet. Maybe He's teaching you to trust in His timing.

37

SOMETHING TO THINK ABOUT . . .

1. Can you recall a time when you prayed for something and God didn't answer you the way you had in mind? Describe it briefly below.

2. Have you had enough time pass to be able to look back and see how God might have worked through your need in a way you did not expect?

3. If we know God always meets our needs, how do we come to grips with the fact that God doesn't always answer our prayers? Do you understand the difference?

4. How does the strength of your relationship with God help pull you through times when it seems God isn't answering your prayers the way you hoped He would?

PAUSE DEVOTION 3

It would be really cool if we could walk and talk with God, wouldn't it?

It would be so easy to have a better relationship with Him if we could just address Him face-to-face. But we can't. We're not Adam or Eve. We can't walk with God through a perfect garden paradise. We're not Abram, or Moses, or Gideon, or Samuel. God (probably) has not appeared to you and talked with you in person. But God gave us His Word to function in much the same way.

You see, God's Word records the shared experiences of God and His people over the course of thousands of years. God inspired people to record these encounters so that all of humankind over the course of time and history would have the Bible as a record of His story.

Through encountering God's Word, we come to know God. We come to know His character. We know how He acts. We know how He works. We learn His plan for us. We learn of His deep, unyielding love for all of humankind. This is the very reason that God gave us His Word . . . so that we might seek and find Him.

How do you know God loves you? Read the Bible.

How do you know the wonderful story of Christ' life, death, and resurrection? Read the Bible.

How do you develop a worldview that sees things such as science, religion, government, finance, environmentalism, and civil rights through the lens of the person of God? Read the Bible!

While it's true that God communicates with us through the Holy Spirit, through creation, through other people, and even through our circumstances, His Word is still His primary means of revealing Himself to His children.

That's why reading Scripture is a vital part of the pause.

SOMETHING TO THINK ABOUT . . .

1. Are you satisfied with your level of devotion to reading God's Word? Are you OK with your current level of understanding of the Bible?

2. In your own words, what are the advantages of knowing the Bible? We've said in *Pause* that it is important. What do you think? Is it? Why?

3. What changes can you make in your daily routine to allow you more time to spend reading the Bible?

PAUSE DEVOTION 4

Paul liked to use the word *ambassador* when he talked about his role in being a servant of Christ. The Greek word he used for ambassador (remember, the New Testament you read is an English translation of a Greek translation) was *presbeutos* pronounced, "pres-BYOO-tahs."

Why the talk of being an ambassador? Because like Paul, you have been charged with being Christ's ambassador. You have been charged with representing the authority and wishes of God. Whoa!

The idea that Paul was communicating when he said "ambassador" is pretty similar to our understanding of it today. Think for a moment about an ambassador to the US from another country, say Azerbaijan or Ethiopia. You may not think you have anything in common with them. But, living your life as an ambassador for Christ is a whole lot more similar to their role than you might expect.

Ambassadors from other countries live and work at their embassies in Washington, D.C. But they are not citizens of the US. They are strangers in a foreign land. **As a Christ-follower, you are called to live in the same way.** You are a representative of Christ. You have to act in a way that tells everyone that your real home is in God's Kingdom, not this world.

Ambassadors are responsible for the honor of their home country. If an ambassador disgraces his or her home country, they are recalled and removed from their position. **You represent Jesus.** Whether you like it or not, people will judge Jesus and His Kingdom by your actions. How you live will either bring honor or dishonor to Jesus, the one who died so that you might live.

Do you see yourself as an ambassador? Well, you are. And you must never forget that to many people, you may be the only "Jesus" they ever see. Do your actions bring glory to God? Or do they take away honor? Don't ever underestimate your influence. More people are watching you than you might realize.

SOMETHING TO THINK ABOUT . . .

1. Be honest: Does this seem fair to you? Does it seem fair that you are judged more strictly than others based on your relationship with Christ?

2. It may not seem fair at times, but if you think about it, it makes a lot of sense. And in some ways, being looked at more closely because you claim to follow Christ can be a good thing. What kinds of opportunities could this open for you?

3. You are God's ambassador. Yes, you. How does that make you feel? How would you describe how effectively you are fulfilling your role?

4. What will it take for you to take your life to the next level? What do you need to do to get more serious about using your life as an asset to God and His mission?

LeaderTreks
YOUTH MINISTRY

HELPING YOUTH WORKERS
MAKE DISCIPLES & DEVELOP LEADERS

RESOURCES | TRAINING | COACHING | TRIPS

877-502-0699
leadertreks.org

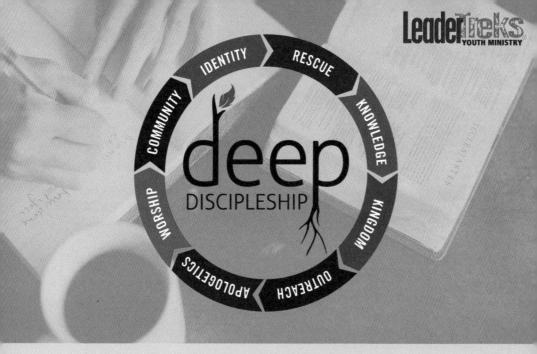

A Multi-Year Curriculum and Strategy for Growing Disciples

A Year-Long Curriculum
Growing Deeply-Rooted Disciples

A Year-Long Curriculum
Focusing on the Actions of Christ

More Deep Discipleship Curriculum at
leadertreks.org/deep-discipleship

ABOUT THE AUTHOR

Andy Blanks is the Co-founder and Publisher for youthministry360. Andy is passionate about God's Word and the transformation it brings in the lives of God's people. What brings Andy the greatest joy is seeing teenagers become sold-out disciples of Christ, following the Lord no matter the cost, and influencing the world around them in the name of Jesus. Andy is a writer, teacher, speaker, and a lifelong Boston Red Sox fan. He lives in Birmingham, AL with his wife, Brendt, and their three daughters and one son.